Wayang

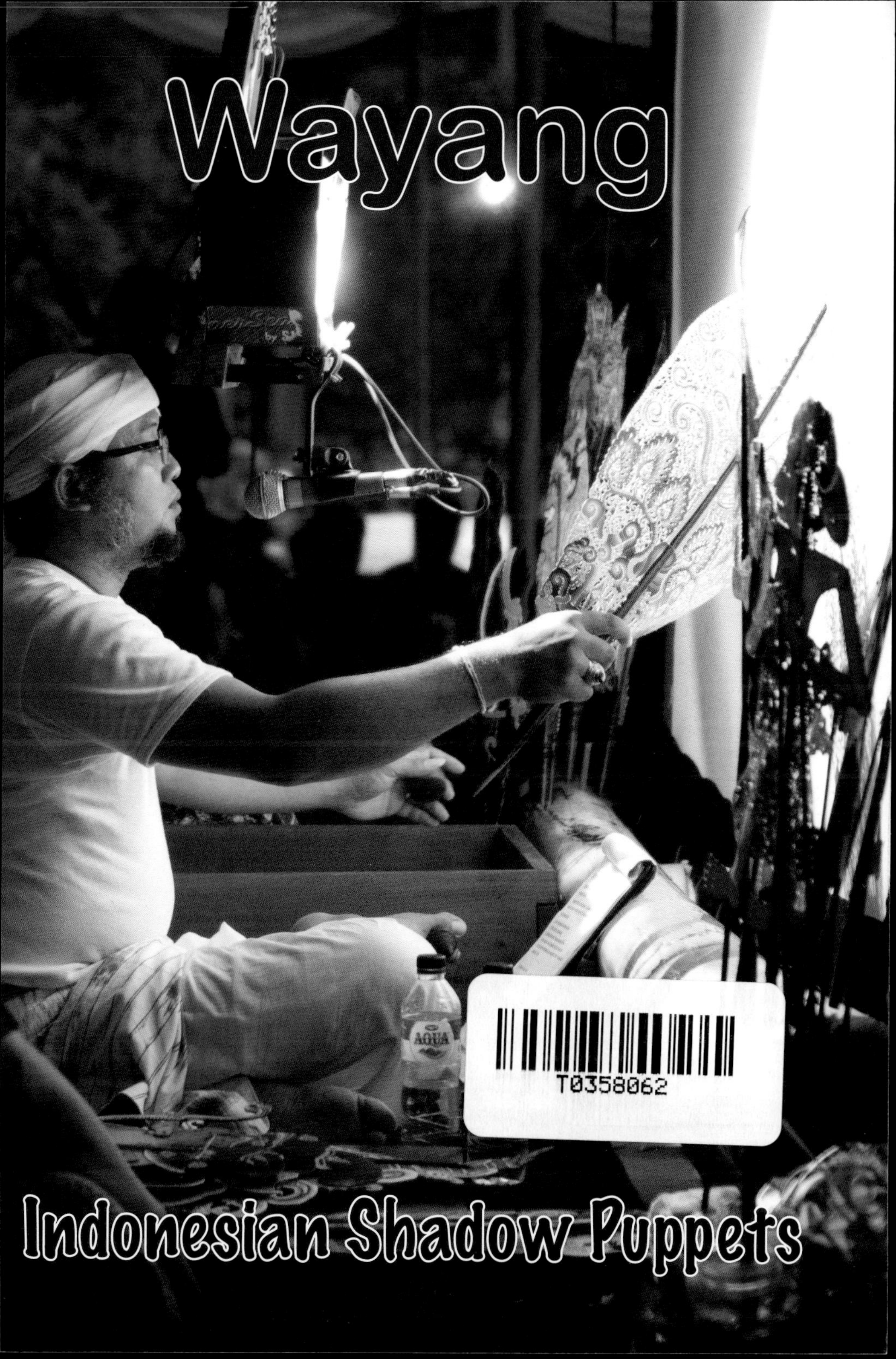

Indonesian Shadow Puppets

Look at the puppet.

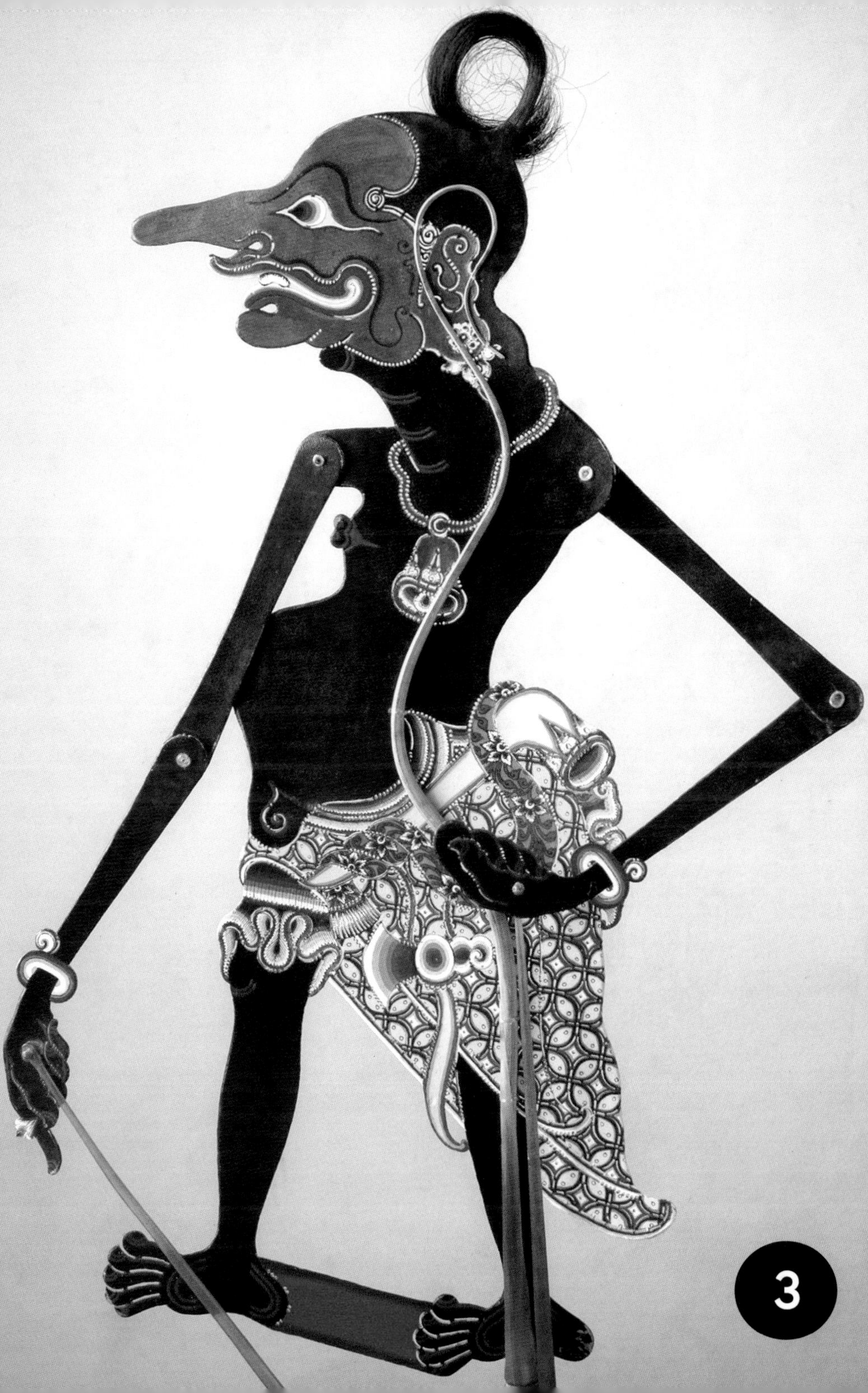

3

Look at the light.

Look at the puppet now.

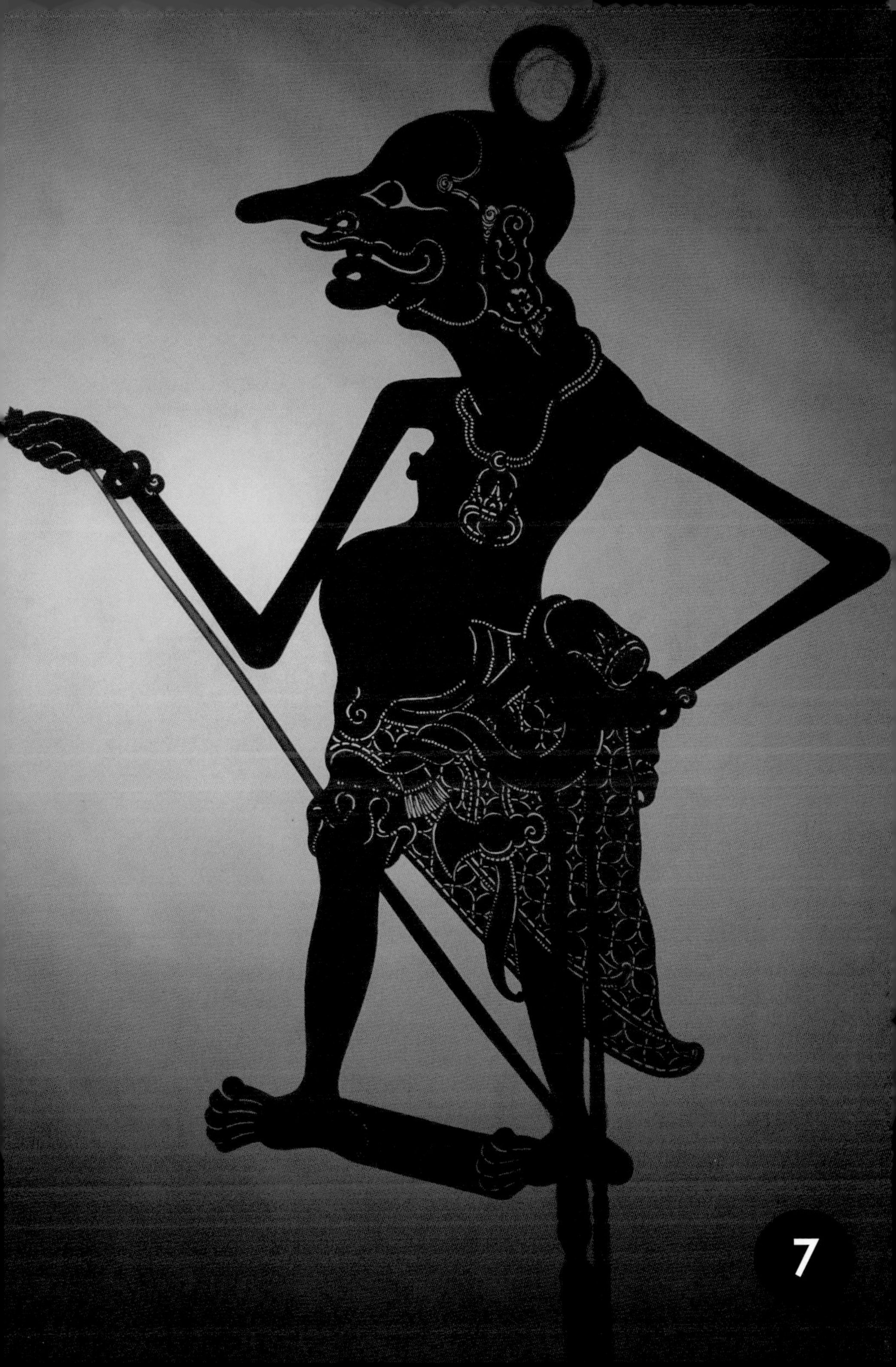

Look at the puppet.

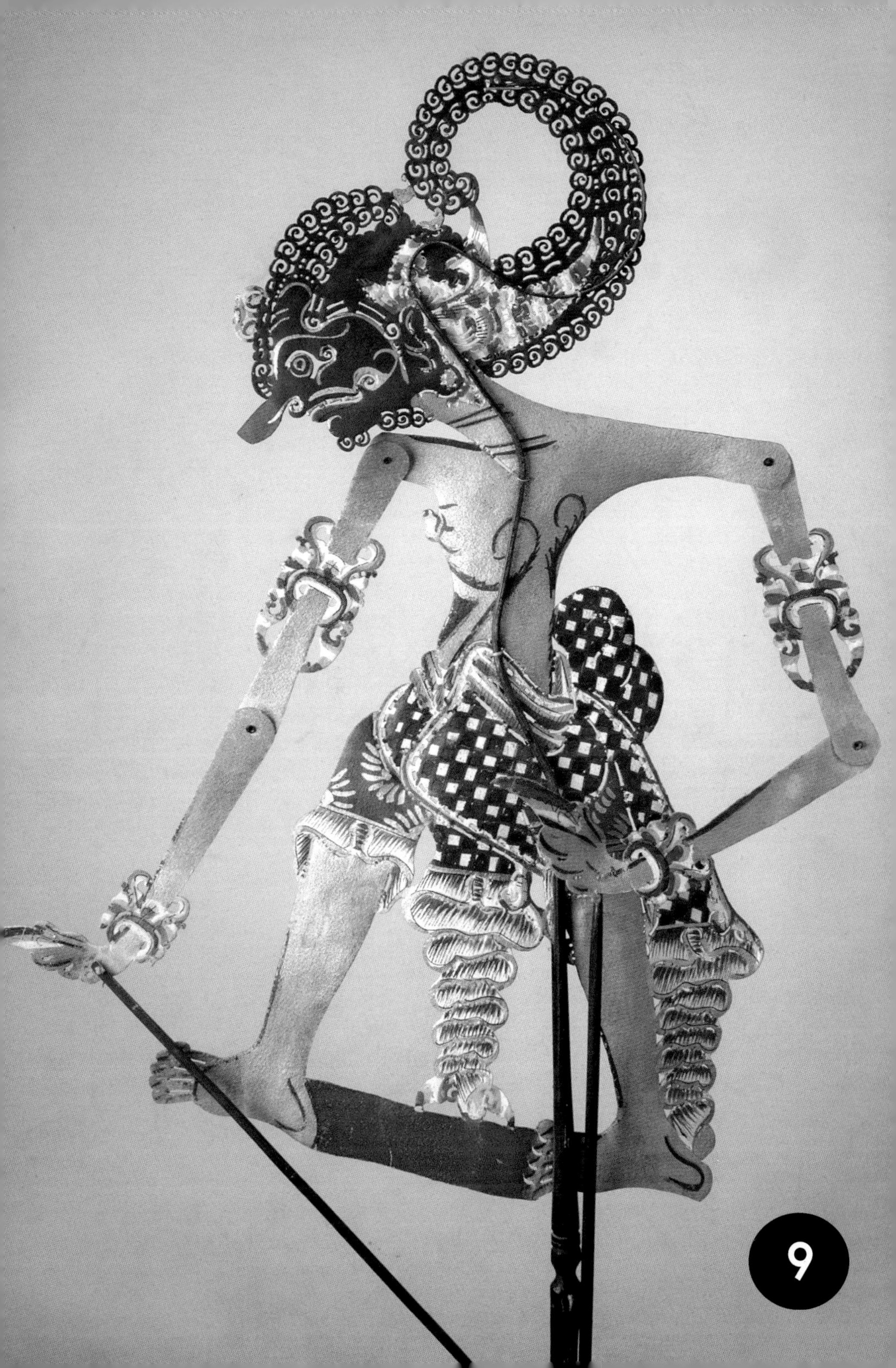
9

Look at the light.

11

Look at the puppet now.

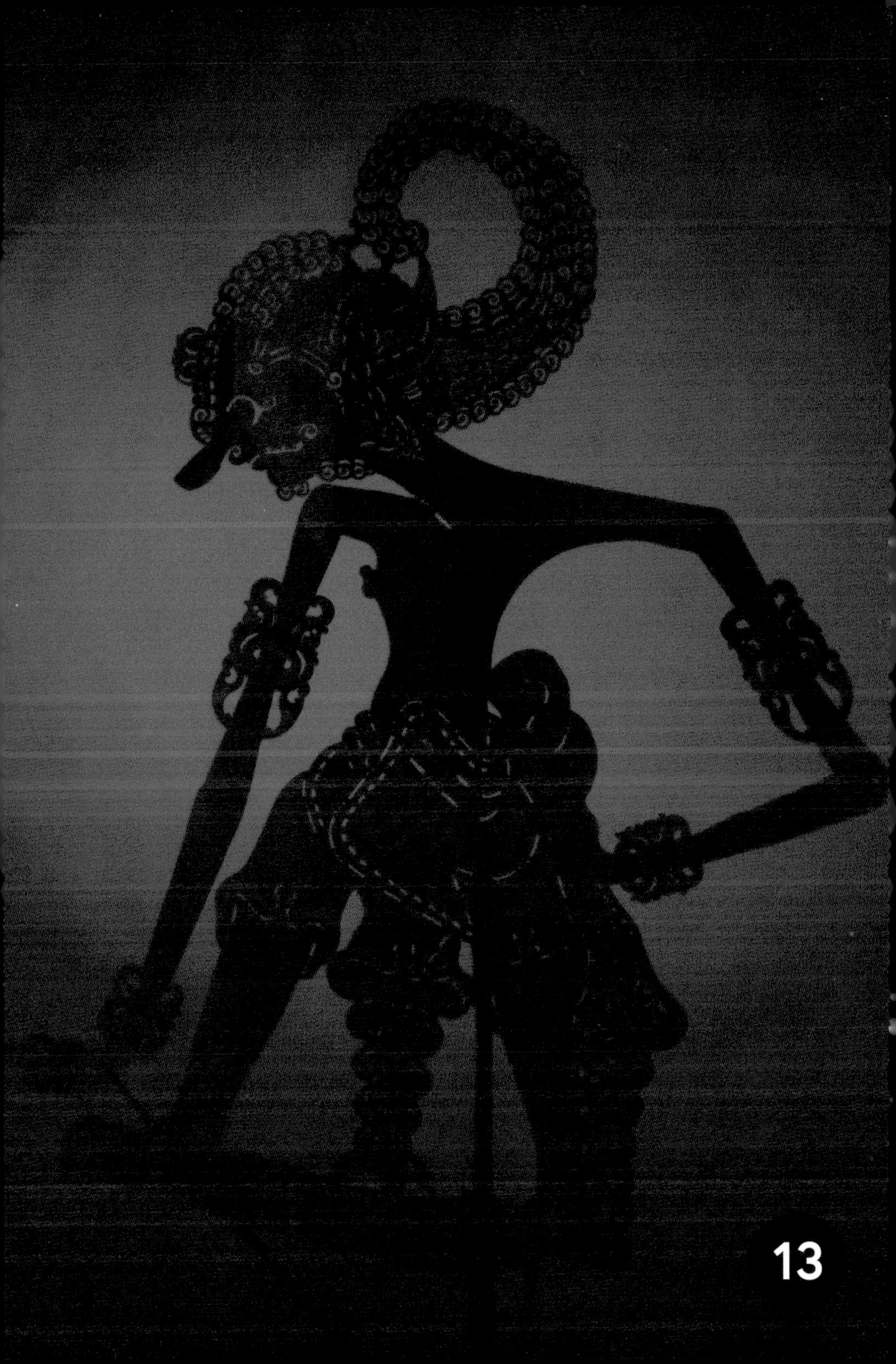

Look at the puppet show!

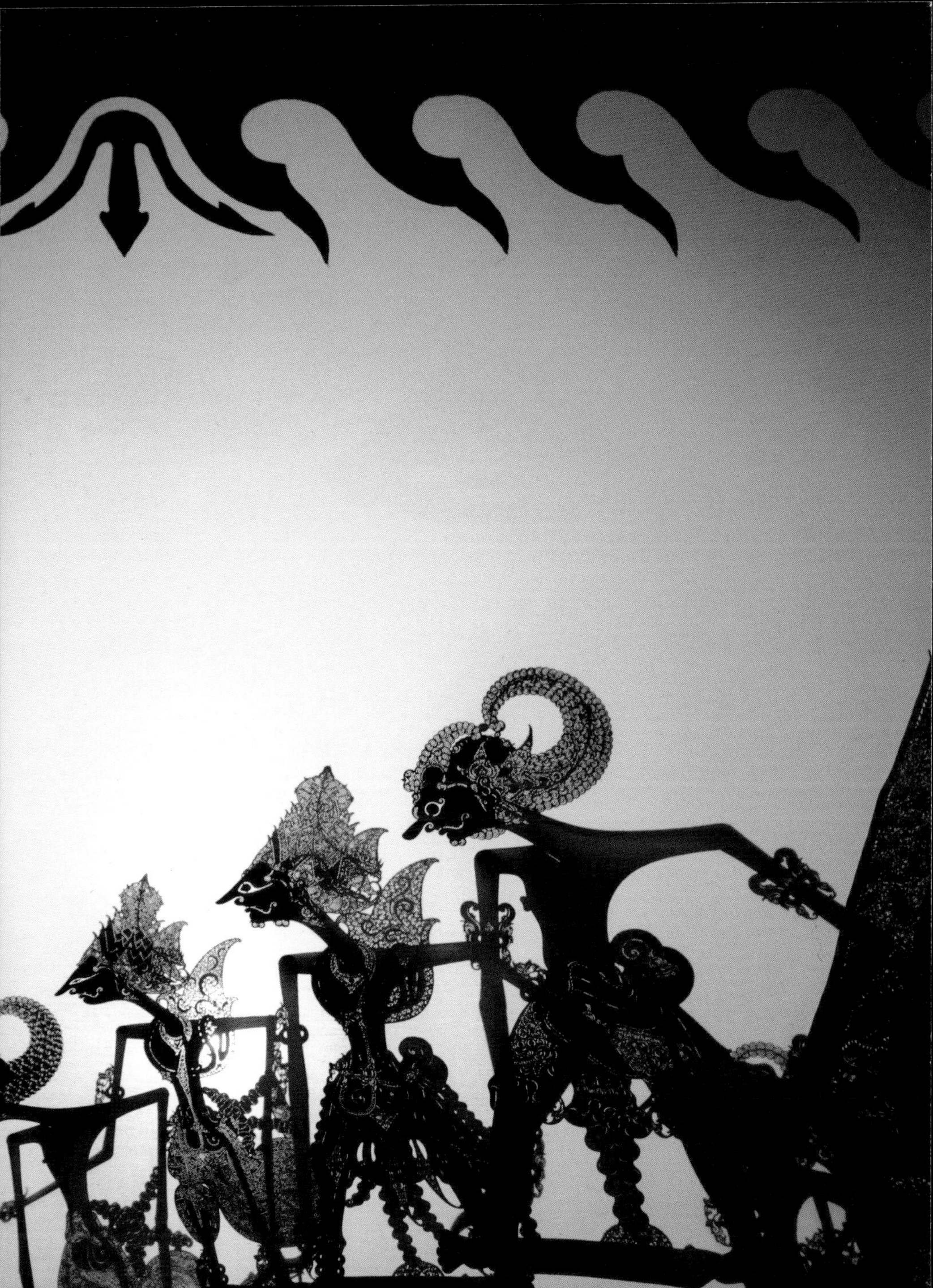

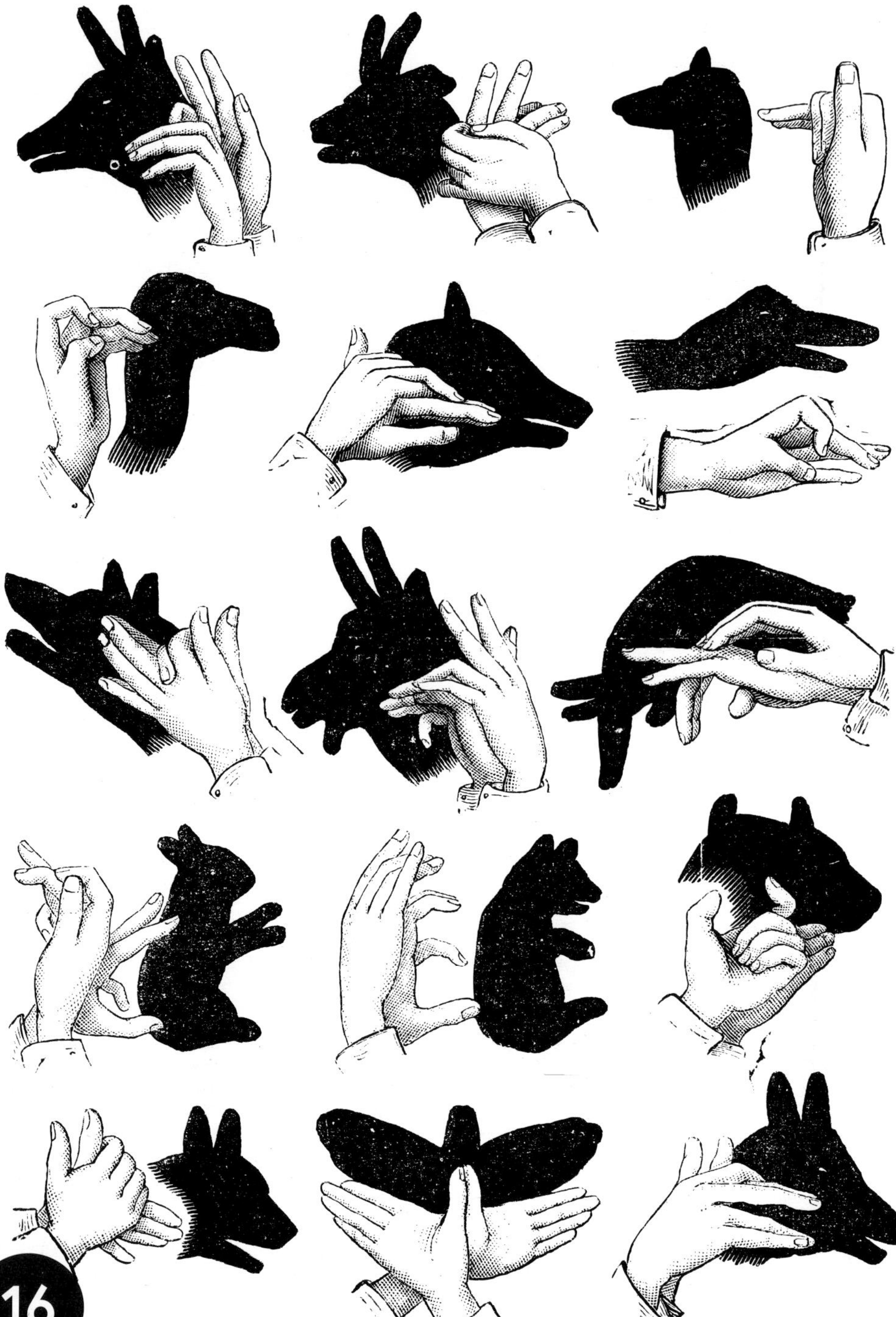